A Guide to Writing Your Memoir or Life Story

Tools, Tips, Methods and Examples

Wayne E. Groner

Paperback-Press
Springfield, Missouri
e-book press publishing - an imprint of A & S Publishing,
A & S Holmes, Inc.
ISBN: 0692419675
ISBN-13: 978-0692419670

There was never yet an uninteresting life.
Such a thing is an impossibility.
Inside of the dullest exterior there is
a drama, a comedy, and a tragedy.

Mark Twain

CONTENTS

ACKNOWLEDGMENTS

Thanks to colleagues and friends who read the manuscript: Larry Cunningham, Eileen Granfors, Jerry-Mac Johnston, Penny Kubitschek, and Linda Thomas. And to my wife, Eryleene. Their recommendations improved the book's accuracy, clarity, and value.

Eryleene provided the cover photo of her Sloan family, circa 1918. Seated, left to right: E.T., her grandfather; Lloyd, a cousin; Martha, her grandmother. Second row, twins Elmer and Edna, her uncle and mother. Back row, left to right: Ruth, Earl, and Charley, her aunt and uncles.

Thanks to those who attended my classes and presentations to community and professional groups. Sometimes cautious, sometimes fearless, their comments contributed to my growing knowledge of the vital work of professional and amateur personal historians, memoirists, and biographers.

7

INTRODUCTION

This book is a guide rather than a comprehensive how-to manual. Just as highway signs and path markers guide you, this book provides markers for your journey. No single book on writing, brief or extensive, will meet all of your needs and answer all of your questions. If, by following these markers, you are motivated to start writing your life story, or to pick up a project you laid aside, then I will have accomplished my purpose.

Be wary of books that promise simple and easy steps, or shortcuts such as completing your story in thirty days or less. There are no simple and easy steps, and *completion* is not possible in that length of time—drafting, yes, but not completion. Writing is long and hard, especially if you are writing for personal or family healing. To do it well requires rewriting, proofreading, editing, doing those multiple times, and getting help from others. David Harrison, award-winning author of children's books, says he rewrote one of his books fifteen times. I say this not to discourage you, but to bring reality to your project.

I hope you enjoy our journey and that it strengthens your resolve to write your story now. Above all, write for yourself, for your enjoyment, to achieve your purposes and not mine or anybody else's. Here's wishing you lots of fun with your project and the best for every success!

VALUE YOUR LIFE STORY

Life story is an umbrella term for memoir, biography, and family history. Memoir is your personal account of experiences over a short period, often pinned to a single event that was a turning point. Biography is your life from birth to today. Family history traces your ancestry from hundreds of years ago to a recent date.

When you write about your life, you risk exposing your vulnerabilities. After all, you can't change the truth; you can only write about the truth as you remember it. That is precisely the point. Your story belongs to you, not anyone else. You own it. You will remember differently, feel differently, and change differently than those who enter and exit your story and those who read it. Give yourself permission to write your story your way.

Bestselling authors seldom come along in any genre,

especially life story writers. When they do, they rarely make a living from book sales; their livelihoods come from speaking, consulting, and teaching. Most people who write their life stories don't expect to become best-selling authors let alone speakers, consultants, or writing teachers. They write for personal satisfaction and to leave a legacy for children and grandchildren to "know it like it was."

"But," you say:

"I'm not a writer."

"I don't know where to begin."

"My family and friends will think I'm conceited."

"Nobody is interested in what I've done."

"There is too much hurt for me to write."

"I can't reveal family secrets."

Those are some of the reasons I hear from students in my writing classes and from attendees at my presentations to professional groups and nonprofits. They are male and female, younger and older, married and single, experienced writers, new writers, and would-be writers. Often, they come with preconceived ideas–obstacles that keep them from starting to write their life stories. Each brings something different while having other things in common. As we work through techniques to help them overcome these obstacles, I impress upon them the most important aspect of writing their life stories is to understand their motivations. "When you know *why* you want to write your story, then you *will be able* to write your story," I tell them.

Common motivations include:
- Leave a family legacy.
- Celebrate charitable or public service.
- Bridge gaps between generations.
- Tell how you went from rags to riches.
- Witness to a life of faith (or struggling to find faith).
- Relate lessons learned from a health tragedy or loss of life.
- Share business advice based on experience.
- Inspire, guide, persuade, influence, empower, teach, or heal.
- Discover one or more purposes in life.
- Make a difference.
- Share stories of romances won or lost, childhood adventures, family fun, or exciting travels.
- Heal your wounds and restore relationships.

Regardless of your experiences and your motivations, your precious memories can become a treasured book for family and friends.

Putting off something is a lot easier than doing it now. The alarm clock goes off at 5:30 a.m. and you press the snooze button several times. Before you know it, it's time for your mid-morning snack and your feet haven't touched the floor; you haven't had breakfast, fed the cat, started the laundry, picked up your prescriptions, or gone on your morning walk in the neighborhood. And why are the children home when it's a school day?

Among the reasons for procrastinating are fear of failure, unclear goals, feeling overwhelmed, and lack of priorities. Putting things off, though, only makes you more uncomfortable.

Years ago in a television commercial on getting started investing, the announcer said, "Today would be fine." In a television commercial for a pizza company, the announcer said gruffly, "Do it!"

You are a part of history, your history that influenced and grew and changed your life and the lives of others. Your life story is important and needs to be shared. Decide now to preserve your precious memories in writing. Put your feet squarely onto the floor, plant your rear firmly into the chair at your computer or with a lined notepad, and start writing.

For a list of websites with dozens of tips to get you started, see **Why You Should Write Your Life Story Now** under **Resources** near the end of this book.

Benefits of Journal Writing

Journal writing has a long history. Famous people who kept journals include Leonardo da Vinci, Lewis Carroll, Andy Warhol, George Bernard Shaw, Anne Frank, L. Frank Baum, and most U.S. presidents.

What is the difference between a journal and a diary? Diary is a record of your experiences and feelings, and many people consider a diary private. Journal also is a record of occurrences and is less personal and more topical such as workout, travel, children, reading inventory, or professional development. Entries in either may be as often as desired.

Journaling can be an excellent way of getting started on your life story. Personal development guru Steve Pavlina says journaling can help with problem solving, improve clarity of thought and expression, and provide markers for determining progress toward your goals.

Besides helping you remember things, journaling causes you to think beyond the act of writing and beyond events you're recording. Benefits include stress management and emotional release, self-discovery, relaxation during quiet time, a learning tool, a teaching tool of medical and academic experts, and an aid to professional and personal growth. Researchers have found that healthy people who journal visit their doctors less often. For those with chronic illnesses, journaling reduces their physical symptoms. Experts declare it to be a gentle and safe therapy.

No right or wrong exists in journaling form or purpose. The important thing is what works for you. I know a journal writer who writes about the day's news events and adds scriptures and references from religious experts to expand or confirm her ethical and moral positions. Some writers use their journaling to interpret dreams to help give meaning to life's uncertainties. Others simply capture events in preparation for someday assembling their notes into a published life story.

Memoirist and workshop presenter Sharon Lippincott says, "Journaling means to me: A place to clear my mind, make my thoughts visible and organize them, and record events. Primarily, it's a place to make sense of life and find deeper meaning. Journaling is my practice, a form of meditation."

You don't have to be a great writer, speller, or creative thinker to journal; just write your thoughts and experiences. You can be as creative and as self-analytical as you wish. No fancy equipment is required. Some journal writers write in longhand in a spiral or three-ring binder, while others write on their computers or online. Others use a bound book of blank pages they carry with them.

You can even give journaling as a gift. Distribute bound journal books with blank pages to members of your family at an annual gathering such as Thanksgiving or Christmas. Invite them to write for one year and then bring the journals to the next gathering for sharing. No requirement for sharing, but you might caution against revealing hurtful or embarrassing details.

THE QUESTION OF
STORY OWNERSHIP

I helped a restaurant owner start writing his life story. He previously published a book on business development and leadership based on lessons learned in the restaurant business and his other successful enterprises including manufacturing, screen-printing, and radio broadcasting.

He wanted to write about the challenges of his personal life including growing up in a dysfunctional family, a failed marriage, rebellious children, and health issues that nearly killed him.

We signed an agreement to conduct recorded interviews weekly, the transcripts of which I edited for his review and approval. After four months, he decided he wanted to go in a different direction. According to our agreement, he paid me for the work I did and I turned over to him all the recordings, transcripts, completed and draft chapters, and file folders of research materials. They belonged to him. This is the proper thing to do and should be stated in a written agreement.

Since 1978 in the United States, copyright occurs immediately when an original work is created and does not depend upon copyright registration. Your book is copyrighted as soon as it is handwritten, in your computer, voice recorded, or captured on video.

On the other hand, by registering your book or recording with the U.S. Copyright Office, you have a legal basis to sue and collect money from anyone who claims your work as his or her own. An application for copyright registration requires a completed application form, a nonrefundable filing fee, and a nonreturnable copy of the work being registered. You may register online or by paper. Online takes eight months or more to receive your certificate of registration, while paper takes thirteen months or more. To register, go to www.copyright.gov and select Register a Copyright. A Copyright Office publication, *Copyright Basics*, is available at www.copyright.gov/circs/circo1.pdf.

To Tell the Truth

A common courtroom oath is, "Do you swear to tell the truth, the whole truth and nothing but the truth, so help you God?" While witnesses may still raise their hands, the use of a Bible in taking the oath generally is out of favor in deference to religious beliefs and the word God deleted for those who object to it.

Rotary International encourages members to use its Four-Way Test in all personal and business matters: "Is it the truth? Is it fair to all concerned? Will it build goodwill and better friendships? Will it be beneficial to all concerned?"

To what extent are writers of life stories required to tell the truth? After all, a life story is a collection of remembrances, not an exercise in journalism. Good stories have conflicts, lessons learned, issues resolved or not, and changes that bring growth. Can a life story writer accurately and fairly remember all those things, especially the dialogue? And do readers really care?

Storytelling has its extremes. Local and regional liars' clubs encourage the telling of tall tales for fun. Mary Karr, in *The Liars' Club: A Memoir*, tells of "a terrific family of liars and drunks" with tidbits and chunks of redeeming truths. Some critics claimed to be unable to tell whether, in some cases, Karr was retelling a fabrication or creating one. She made up the name Leechfield, Texas, as her hometown, probably to spare the feelings of residents of her real hometown because of the gritty and raw nature of her childhood.

James Frey was embarrassed by national media when the media revealed much of his bestseller, *A Million Little Pieces*, was made up. Oprah Winfrey initially praised him and then publicly rebuked him for lying.

Some books and movies declare to be based on true stories. *Based on* are the operative words. In many cases the opening credits should include, "Some of the following is true."

Does life story qualify as creative nonfiction, that ambiguous and relatively new term for using fiction-writing techniques to tell true stories? Supporters hold creative nonfiction encourages personal viewpoint and conjecture, a position that is true of memoir. Author and memoir writing coach Denis Ledoux contends there is a clear difference between memoir—remembering and reacting to facts—and autobiographical fiction which is plot driven.

Ben Yagoda and Dan DeLorenzo, writing for the Nieman Storyboard project at Harvard University, declared simple answers are not available for the complex questions surrounding truth in memoirs. Although their research focused on memoir, it could apply to all life story types.

They tried to take on the problems of memoir inaccuracies by constructing a scoring system, a system they admit is half-facetious and half-serious. They rate inaccuracies according to their negative reflections on people, living or dead; corroboration of facts; questionable dialogue; clichés and flat writing; and self-deprecation. A passing score is 65 out of 100.

They applied their scoring to nine memoirs from the year 397 CE to 2009 CE. Ernest Hemingway's *A Movable Feast* received a 69, James Frey's *A Million Little Pieces* got 29, and Sarah Palin's *Going Rogue: An American Life* got 69. Read the full scoring report at http://tinyurl.com/pupjvza and download a printable worksheet to evaluate your memoir. It is a subjective process, since we are all biased about our own work, but it could prove insightful.

What does all this mean for you? If you want to be accepted and respected then you must be as accurate and truthful as possible. What does it mean for today's readers who are the final judges because they approve or reject books based on what they buy? As Yagoda and DeLorenzo said, ". . . an informed reader has to make the call."

WORKING WITH
A PERSONAL HISTORIAN

Outsourcing is a common business practice. Companies feel their time, staff, equipment, and money are better spent on what they do best. They pay companies with expertise in other areas to handle narrowly defined assignments.

Many people outsource the expertise needed to help them write their life stories. They don't know how to begin writing or they don't have the time, so they engage a personal historian.

A personal historian helps you write your memories. He or she records interviews with you and writes and edits a narrative based on the interviews. The project can include selecting and formatting photos, designing and laying out a book, printing and distributing the book, producing a DVD, or creating a family website. Some functions may be contracted to other vendors. You review and approve the final product and receive a copy of the work.

You may include anything in your narrative. It can be a few stories of key events in your life or it can encompass your entire life. Major areas often are childhood, adolescence, young adulthood and married life, and elder years. Before beginning a project, decide the extent of information you want to include and whether you will be doing genealogy searches. A note of caution on genealogy: It can go on forever. Unless you are extremely knowledgeable and experienced in this area or can engage someone who is, I recommend you stick to straight narrative. Not all personal historians will do genealogies.

Another note: Your name will appear in the book as author; your personal historian is your ghostwriter. Whether you credit your ghostwriter on the cover and title page or on your acknowledgements page, or give no credit, is something you work out with the ghostwriter. Some ghostwriters don't care whether they receive credit, while others may reduce their fees in return for credit.

The cost of working with a personal historian depends on what you want in the final product, which determines how much work a ghostwriter will do for you. An experienced personal historian will conduct an initial consultation with you at no cost and then prepare a detailed written agreement on what he or she will do, including a period to complete the project and what is expected of you. Family members may participate in the costs or commission a project for a loved one. Personal historians may charge by the hour or by the project. The interview process could take a dozen hours or more, usually in several sessions of one hour to ninety minutes each. Your personal historian then transcribes the recordings and writes the narrative. Writing can take ten times as long as the interviews. Then comes editing and shaping the final manuscript for your approval and the production of a book or video as you direct.

Out-of-pocket expenses may be incurred for transportation, lodging, food, and telephone. You work out with your personal historian whether these are additional charges or whether they will be rolled into a package price. An experienced personal historian will not be able to do a well-crafted personal history for $1,000. Typically, projects cost $5,000 to $10,000 and can go over $50,000.

For more information:
- Visit your library to find out whether a writers' group is in your area. Some members may be personal historians or can direct you to one.
- Type the words *personal historian* into your Web browser's search field.
- Visit the Association of Personal Historians, http://www.personalhistorians.org/.

NOTES

WRITE CLEARLY TO BE EFFECTIVE

I love this quote; it keeps me on track when my sentences get long and my meanings hazy: "It is not enough we write to be understood. We must write so we cannot possibly be misunderstood."

Variations of the quote on the Internet are attributed to Robert Louis Stevenson, and if it's on the Internet it must be correct, right? "I'm pretty sure this is not by Stevenson," says Richard Dury, author of books on Stevenson and co-founder of international conferences on Stevenson. Shucky darn. That won't stop me from using the quote; I'll just have to qualify it.

The intent of the quote is evident in governments and corporations making extra efforts to write laws, instructions, and contracts in plain language. Some succeed better than others. The Centers for Medicare & Medicaid Services (CMS) has a free download, "Toolkit for Making Written Material Clear and Effective." While the guidelines are intended for those who write for the needs of CMS audiences, they are an excellent resource for families, friends, community organizations, and life story writers. The principles for clear and effective communications apply to any writer for any audience.

The toolkit has a table of contents and eleven parts. The parts may be downloaded as a complete set or separately. Topics include using a reader-centered approach, guidelines for writing and design including the Web, materials for older adults, and a section of before-and-after examples.

The toolkit includes examples for "brochures and pamphlets, booklets, flyers, fact sheets, posters, bookmarks, application forms, comparison charts, postcards, instruction sheets, and questionnaires." The examples can be applied to any type of writing.

The toolkit cautions on using grade-level readability formulas which "are used to measure difficulty of vocabulary and sentences in written materials," stating such formulas tend to be narrow and limiting.

In the section titled "Guidelines for Writing," the toolkit includes how-to-do-it information on what readers want and need to know, using plenty of headings and subheadings, pacing readers, using an active voice, and using a conversational style.

In the section titled "Material for Older Adults," the

toolkit includes information on how aging affects literacy skills, helping those with vision limitations, and helping those with declining cognitive skills.

Download the written materials toolkit at http://tinyurl.com/6mb97vb.

NOTES

TECHNIQUES FOR
GATHERING INFORMATION

Here are three techniques for gathering information for your life story. I interviewed each of these persons to learn their methods for journaling, drawing on experiences and family records, and recording interviews.

Technique One – Journaling

Mike and Cindy Schaffer,
The Best We Remember

Mike and Cindy Schaffer have a treasured written record of many things their children said and did while growing up. They started writing one month after their son Ryan (Rynie) was born in 1981 and continued when their son Aaron (Tow, pronounced

TOE) was born in 1986.

Mike and Cindy are retired from the state of Missouri. She was a secretary and he was an employment counselor.

"When I went to work, I wrote the children's activities and sayings on my desk calendar just about every day," Mike says. "At the end of the day, I tore off the calendar page and brought it home, where I kept the pages wrapped in a rubber band in a drawer. If something happened over the weekend, I would try to remember it and write it on the calendar when I got back to work."

The first entry, December 17, 1981: "Babysitter said Ryan gagged himself trying to chew on his fingers. Wanted to be held all evening. Ate his cereal well. May be getting his appetite back after his first shot."

December 29, 1981: "Got three bright toys for Christmas. Beads, key ring, train. He notices them now. Using his hands some now to grab and move them, but they usually end up in his mouth. Rolls over on his side. Looks intently at the bumper cars and the figures. Makes a lot more noise. Cackles, moans, grunts, whines and cries more than he once did."

Both boys had their special blankets when they were little. Mike recalls one morning when Tow was five years old and he got him up for the day that Tow had tied his blanket into a knot. That night when Tow went to bed with his blanket, he said, "It's not useful that way."

Also when Tow was five, Mike wrote Tow was disappointed that Rynie got new soccer shoes and he didn't. "My shoes are junk," Tow said.

Seeing a stalled car at the side of a street, Rynie said, "They wore out their gas."

Watching the movie *Dancing with Wolves* with Cindy when a nude scene came up, Rynie said, "Mom, do you like this movie?"

Tow: "Will you keep an ear on me while I swim?"

When Cindy told Rynie that tofu comes from bean curd, he said, "Where is that?"

Tow's description of a fried egg: "Put it in a pan and don't bother it. And it makes a yellow lump."

Rynie, when he wanted his dad to take him fishing: "Dad, you've lived a long time, so you should know how to fish by now."

The last entries in the journal were in 1995 when Rynie was fourteen years old and Tow was nine. "It was a time when their interests were turning to friends and school activities, so it was good time for us to stop," Mike says. Today, Rynie is married, and he and his wife enjoy reading the journal. They have a son. "He is very much like his father," Mike says.

"I love the journal," Cindy says. "I would never have

remembered all of those things if Mike hadn't done that."

"It's priceless," Mike says.

When Cindy and Mike retired, Cindy transcribed the calendar notes to a computer and added pictures of the boys. She included some scanned items in the boys' handwriting, including a letter Tow wrote from Bible camp and a short story by Rynie. The final eight-and-a-half-by-eleven memoir totals seventy-seven pages. They took the pages to a quick-print shop for binding in a plastic spiral with a clear plastic cover and had several copies printed. They titled it, *The Best We Remember*.

Technique Two – Drawing on Experiences and Family Records

Todd Parnell's Three Memoirs

Former Drury University President Todd Parnell didn't write for money. He wrote to enjoy, to honor his family's legacy, and to give back to the community, passionate motivations strongly evident in his three captivating family memoirs. Proceeds from two of the books go to nonprofits and have provided them with more than $50,000.

He wrote his books the old-fashioned way: with pen and pad.

Mom at War
Todd's mother, Jean, became a war widow in 1943
when her first husband was killed in Sicily. She
joined the American Red Cross to honor his
memory, and in 1944 and 1945 drove a two-ton truck
across Germany giving doughnuts, coffee, and com-
fort to our front-line troops.

"She never provided details of her experiences to me
and my brother, Patrick," Todd says.

Jean gave up her secrets more than fifty years after
the war when she showed Todd a wooden German
ammunition box full of her letters, photographs, di-
aries, and other memorabilia. Materials included,
accounts of witnessing airplane dogfights, surviving
a bombing of her quarters and strafing of her truck
by enemy aircraft, suffering frostbite, and being at
the Battle of the Bulge.

Todd turned the materials into *Mom at War*. He
gave a copy to his parents, Jean and Ben, during a
Mother's Day lunch. Proceeds from book sales go to
the Greater Ozarks Regional Chapter of the American Red Cross and to the Southwest Missouri Chapter of the Alzheimer's Association.

*Postcards from Branson: A Century of Family
Reminiscence*
Todd's father, grandfather, and great-grandfather
grew up in Branson, Missouri. They were bankers
who were leaders of progress and action. Branson
also was where Todd and Patrick were raised, so it
was natural for Todd to want to write about the

area.

"This book was more difficult to organize than *Mom at War*," Todd says. "Materials were not kept in a single box; they were in many boxes in a basement. My family kept every scrap of paper they touched, so the materials were a treasure trove of documented memories."

Where to start? An opening occurred when Todd's parents invited him and Patrick on a cruise without their wives so they could spend some private time together. Todd quizzed his parents almost daily during the cruise on what they remembered about Branson. It was many years later that he returned to his notes and compared them with the photos, articles, and other materials in the basement boxes, piecing together the stories that became this book.

"I'm proud of the stories of my kinfolks," Todd says. "They're not famous and nobody's going to write those things for them. I wanted to do that. The book also lets my children know about our roots."

He gave his parents a copy of *Postcards from Branson*, an emotional moment for everyone since by that time his father was in a skilled nursing home. His parents passed away a few years later. Proceeds from book sales go to Cox Medical Center South, Branson.

The Buffalo, Ben and Me

Todd framed this book around a twelve-day float trip on the Buffalo National River in Arkansas with his son Ben, who was in the eighth grade and struggling with learning challenges.

"He was not performing at his potential and that made him resentful," Todd says.

The wilderness adventure changed their lives and strengthened their love as Todd helped his son gain self-confidence and searched for his own identity as a father. They became more connected with every navigated rapid, every passage through massive limestone bluffs, every bass caught, and every glimpse of a deer, turkey, turtle and snakes–lots of snakes.

Todd started writing about the trip as soon as they got home. "We both did a lot of growing, and I wanted to make sure those memories didn't slip away."

Ben received professional counseling in high school that helped match his needs with learning resources. He went on to receive a master's degree in biology with a focus on fisheries management and work for the Missouri Department of Conservation.

Todd plans to keep writing until things are so dim in his head he can't think of any words.

Technique Three – Recording Interviews

Tony and Sandra's Unfinished Project

Interviewing elderly persons can have a different set

of challenges than younger persons. Elderly persons may be frail, drowsy, forgetful, and struggling with age-related illnesses. Interviews tend to be in shorter time segments. Husband and wife Sandra and Tony learned elderly spouses interviewed together often have conflicting remembrances of the same events, and family members may not be on board with the project.

"David and Martha have been very special to us," Sandra says. "David was our pastor for several years, a lay minister, and a retired dairy farmer. Martha had been an Avon Lady. God helped them bless hundreds, if not thousands, of people through their humble ministries. The record of their lives is truly a journey in the hand of the Master."

Sandra and Tony heard the testimonies of David and Martha over many years and felt the stories should be captured permanently for family and friends.

"David carried on daily conversations with the Lord that guided his every step," Tony says.

Tony had no training in writing memoirs when he met with David and Martha in 2008 to discuss recording and writing their memories.

"They were very receptive," he says. "They were in their eighties, and Martha had wanted to do something like this but felt she couldn't pull it off because she was not computer literate. We agreed I would come to their house every Tuesday night to record. Sandra would transcribe the recordings into a computer and do the editing."

Sandra and Tony thought it might take a dozen interviews. The project lasted two years.

The first few months went very well, although it was hard to keep David from jumping around from topic to topic. "If you asked him what time it was he would tell you how to build a watch," Tony quips. "He was never shy; humble, but not shy. Once we got him talking we pretty much sat back and listened."

The interviews became less productive as David and Martha had strong words over which details went with which stories. It was helpful that David kept a notebook of his many activities, including funeral services at which he officiated, spiritual experiences, and testimonies. Still, he and Martha disagreed.

"Sandy gave them a draft to read and they radically changed it," Tony says. "More drafts and more changes followed. Discussions on the changes took longer than the interviews. David and Martha couldn't agree on whether an event occurred west of town or east, whether it was in May or August. Our progress was minimal."

Adding to the frustration was the deteriorating health of the elderly couple, including poor hearing, reduced eyesight, and David's ongoing battle with arthritis. The transcriptions had to be printed in eighteen-point type.

After two years, Sandra and Tony felt they had done as much as they could with the narrative. They printed the stories into a two-hundred page, double-spaced manuscript and gave it to a son and daughter of David and Martha to determine what the next steps might be. The children had sat in on some of the interviews.

"Our thinking was for the manuscript to be at least in a spiral binding and copies printed to give to family and friends," Sandra says. "The children were going to gather pictures and prepare a family tree."

The children were not excited about distributing the manuscript as written. They were concerned about how some people might feel having their names and personal stories in print. They wanted Sandra and Tony to provide the manuscript on a CD and that would be the end of the project.

"There was nothing offensive to anybody," Tony says. "When you take the names and places out, the story is gutted. The children may have thought the project was just something to keep Mom and Dad occupied, a good activity to keep their minds active. We were disappointed the record of this man's walk with the Lord would be shared with only the family, and we consider the project to be unfinished; no wrap-up, no conclusion."

Sandra and Tony say they learned the importance of getting up-front confirmation from the family on whether the manuscript will be formatted as a book, what the review process will be, what the final work will look like, and who will be responsible for printing and costs.

"Most important, we learned we should have started the project much sooner," Sandra says.

David and Martha are living their remaining years in a nursing home.

David and Martha are not their real names.

Other information-gathering techniques

Your librarian can direct you to resources, including books similar to what you plan to write as well as cultural, social, and historical volumes for adding authentic details. Some libraries have free access for members to Ancestry.com, where you can find U.S. census records and records of marriages, births, and deaths. You may obtain your own paid subscription. Many libraries have local and area newspapers on microfilm.

Online sites offer paid subscriptions for family research, including searches of newspapers, passengers arriving in the U.S. by ship from other countries, and searches by nationality. *About.com* offers free newsletters on writing memoirs and on genealogy research; scroll to the bottom of its home page for a list of categories.

NOTES

GOOD BOOK DESIGN IS ESSENTIAL

A book that looks like a book will maintain a place of honor on a bookshelf or coffee table and is more likely to be shared with others as an important work the author, family members, and friends are proud to own.

Print-on-demand (POD) companies using digital technologies will easily and affordably print your manuscript with the look and feel of books produced by major publishing companies. Some POD vendors will print as few as one book; others have minimums of ten copies, twenty-five copies, or other amounts.

The costs of using a POD are wide-ranging, beginning at zero per book at *CreateSpace.com* and *Lulu.com.* Final costs are determined by your choices of softcover or hardcover, use of color, number of pages, copies printed, and additional services such as layout, photo placement, cover design, proofreading, editing, and marketing. Shipping is additional.

Some PODs have online templates for you to layout your book and design your front cover and back cover at no extra charge. You could pay the POD to do it, or engage a local or online artist who is experienced at cover designing.

Advantages of POD over traditional publishing include lower start-up costs, minimal or no book storage, no struggling to find a publisher or agent, and complete control by the author. Disadvantages include a perception of less prestige, which is diminishing because of the explosive growth of POD; limited shelf exposure by traditional bookstores; and author takes on all risks and costs of design, printing, distribution, promotion, and sales.

You can design your book with Microsoft Word templates from *Self-Publishing, Inc.*, http://tinyurl.com/8y9796z; *Book Design Templates*, http://tinyurl.com/owqf2ha; and *Jera Publishing*, http://tinyurl.com/qhoh2zm. For more options, search your browser for *book design templates*, *print on demand*, or *manuscript formatting*.

In recent years, hybrid go-between vendors have emerged who will set up and publish your book using *CreateSpace.com* and *Lulu.com*, so you don't have to learn the process, which can be intimidating. A hybrid vendor published this book. The hybrids are neither POD companies nor traditional publishers, and their fees often are much lower. You are not required to purchase a minimum number of books, you retain complete artistic control, and you keep all royalties and profits. Many of the hybrids work out of residences and are visible only by their websites and networking. Search your browser for *manuscript preparers* or *book layout vendors*. Ask your librarian, writers' group, or English Department head at a college or university for possible contacts.

When researching companies, ask to see a sample copy of a book similar to yours. Check for quality of paper, layout, professional-looking typestyles, and how well photos are reproduced.

NOTES

WRITING YOUR STORY: 12 TIPS

The Bible is a compilation of books written over centuries by different persons for different reasons. It is the foundation for millions (I haven't counted them) of books, research papers, and movies on characters who roamed through history and religion.

Cecil B. DeMille is supposed to have said, "Give me any page in the Bible and I will give you a movie." Three of the world's great religions trace their histories to Abraham in the Old Testament: Islam, Judaism, and Christianity. Books of the Bible are examples of the basic life story types of memoir, biography, and family history, as well as the varied approaches writers took to the same story such as the gospels.

Regardless of the life story type you decide to write, these tips will help you clarify how you present your story to readers.

1. **Decide the type of life story you will write: memoir, biography, or family history.** You have two options in making this decision: write without categorizing the type, freeing you from artificial boundaries, or determine the type before you begin. Knowing enables you to focus within a framework that keeps you from wandering in uncontrolled directions, and it defines your parameters for research. Yes, you'll have to do research. Dagnabbit. Your story set in Cairo, Illinois will be different than if set in Cairo, Egypt.

Regardless of the type of life story you write, good storytelling is essential. A good story has a beginning, middle, and ending, characters readers relate to whether they love them or hate them, and conflicts which may or may not be resolved. I recommend to students in my classes and to clients they decide the type of life story before they begin. By limiting their scope, they can focus on their stories rather than fantasize about getting an agent, a big publishing advance, having a best-selling book, and becoming famous.

Examples of memoir, biography, and family history.
The basic types of life story writing are distinguished mainly by time. Biography is from birth

to today. It is a biography if you write about someone else and an autobiography if you write about yourself. Celebrities and politicians often are subjects of biographies and autobiographies.

Memoir covers a short time period or series of related events such as childhood, teenage years, military service, trauma, spiritual journey, and so forth. Your stories tell key experiences that influenced you and how you changed. Examples: *Growing Up Amish* by Ira Wagler, *The Liars' Club* by Mary Karr, and *Because I Remember Terror, Father, I Remember You*, by Sue Williams Silverman.

Family history uses genealogy, photos, and stories to tell about your ancestors. You may start several centuries ago and stop at any date you choose. Examples: *Sloan and Related Families*, about my wife's family from 1756 to today; and husband and wife Dawn and Morris Thurston, each of whom wrote a family history.

Not all life stories fit neatly into the three types. *Esther: The Remarkable True Story of Esther Wheelwright*, is as much about author Julie Wheelwright's journey to learn about an ancestor as it is about the ancestor. Esther was a mother superior who saved her convent in the 1759 English siege of Quebec City, Canada. Books of the Bible are mixtures of life story types. The variety of biblical authors did not write to illustrate types, but to show God's compassion to humans with stories told through laws, history, wisdom, prophecies, hymns, poetry, and letters.

2. Define your motivation for writing your life story.

All creatures feel the need to be connected, whether honeybees or humans, wolves or whales, amoebae or anteaters; whether by village, tribe, pack, household, school, work, neighborhood, city, county, state, country, religion, or politics. Realize it or not, in writing your life story you have a need to be connected.

Identify your need

Psychologist Abraham Maslow (1908-1970) created a five-stage hierarchy of needs. Other researchers expanded Maslow's work into seven and eight stages. Maslow's stages in order of importance are survival, protection, belonging, self-esteem, and personal growth. A dependency factor is common to all stages—humans need to be connected. If you were to trace any household object, such as a pencil or ballpoint pen, from your house back to a retail store, distribution center, manufacturer, raw materials, and so forth, you would discover this dependency in thousands, if not millions, of lives.

Define your motivation for writing—the reason or reasons you want to be connected—and you will be able to write. Do you want to become famous? Make loads of money? Find personal enjoyment? Honor family legacy? Give back to the community? Help your children and grandchildren understand and appreciate their heritage? Find personal or family healing? Share your journey of faith to inspire others? Set the record straight? Think about all the connections within those questions.

Find your passion

Marriage and family therapist, author, and memoir writing instructor Linda Joy Myers puts it this way: "The most important ingredient in writing a memoir is motivation–a passionate reason to get the story on the page, a 'fire in the belly' feeling that what you have to tell is important and significant."

The foundational theme for your connections enables you to construct the narrative of your life story. Is your theme travel, nostalgia, war, public or celebrity life, humor, charity or service, personal struggles, spiritual faith found or lost, surviving loss of a loved one, social or cultural issues, advice based on experience, confessional, coming of age, rags to riches, dysfunctional family, romance, or trauma? Myriad themes are available, even revenge with caution.

Revenge is not a good reason to write your life story. It might make an exciting fiction book or movie, but don't use it as your life story to get back at someone; that only perpetuates your hurts and theirs. It's okay to write about revenge as a teaching and learning tool, says Marion Roach Smith in her *The Memoir Project: A Thor-*

oughly Non-Standardized Text for Writing & Life, but don't use your story as a weapon.

Learn from athletes
Television commercials have shown aspiring Olympians become motivated by watching winning Olympians and noting their times or scores. The Olympians-to-be wrote the times in dirt or sand, or on a note attached to a refrigerator door.

Write your motivation on a sticky note and attach it to your computer screen or refrigerator, or write it on the cover of a spiral notebook. It's okay to have more than one motivation, but more than three muddies your focus and can be overwhelming. Think about what you want to accomplish with your life story. Think of the benefits of the results of your published work. Think of how your life story will make a difference, not only in your life but also in the lives of those who read it.

3. **Read stories you enjoy and follow their approaches.**
    At the start of each of my life story writing classes, I ask students why they came. What is bothering you about writing? What has kept you from starting or completing your memoir, biography, or family history? I write their answers on a whiteboard and then turn the list out of view. At the end of class, we revisit the list to see whether we covered their concerns.

Concerns include where to begin, what to do about painful memories, will I be sued, fears of what family or friends will say, I'm not a writer, and who will want to read it. A top concern: How do I make my story interesting?

Do this and you can't miss
The best way to make your life story interesting, that is, write so people will want to read it, is to pay attention to how others write. You do that by reading stories you enjoy: nonfiction, short stories, poems, essays, mystery novels, romances, action-adventures, memoirs, biographies, and so on. You can learn from the myriad of mentors, models, and methods that made others successful. Lee Iacocca is believable in *Where Have All the Leaders Gone?* because he was president of Ford Motor Company, Chrysler Corporation, and headed the Statue of Liberty-Ellis Island Foundation (his parents were Italian immigrants). Stephen King is believable in *On Writing: A Memoir of the Craft* because he wrote more than fifty novels that sold millions of copies. Literary agent Paula Balzer is believable in *Writing & Selling Your Memoir* because she represented best-selling authors.

Choose your favorites
Pick any author and genre: The late Ray Bradbury's science fiction, William Zinsser's nonfiction, Cait London's romances, James Patterson's thrillers, or whatever you like. Buy at random a handful of cheap paperbacks at a used-book sale. Browse books in your library. Read them. Pay at-

tention to how authors construct a scene, develop conflict, write dialogue, present character traits, show action, and use other good storytelling techniques. When you find yourself drawn into the plot and into the lives of characters, real or fiction, pay attention to how the author took you there. Soon you will say, "I can write like that."

Reading, learning, applying keep you engaged in your craft. Practice writing a few paragraphs or a chapter of your own story in the style of a favorite author. This was carried to extreme by Yoknapatawpha Press, which for many years sponsored the Faux Faulkner Contest, now suspended. Yoknapatawpha County, Mississippi, is a fictional place created by William Faulkner (1897-1962), who was a native of Mississippi.

"Read, read, read," Faulkner said. "Read everything–trash, classics, good and bad, and see how they do it. Just like a carpenter who works as an apprentice and studies the master. Read! You'll absorb it."

Stephen King said, "If you want to be a writer, you must do two things above all other: read a lot and write a lot."

4. **Focus on key events by making a list of memory joggers.**
    Memory joggers are writing prompts. Use them to speed up your writing process and free your mind to write. Your goal in listing memory jog-

gers is not perfection in details; it is to remember that events occurred.

You could outline your entire life story using memory joggers, similar to the approach Linda Spence takes in *Legacy: A Step-by-step Guide to Writing Personal History*. She divides a life into nine major segments: beginnings and childhood, adolescence, early adult years, marriage, being a parent, middle adult years, being a grandparent, later adult years, and reflections. In each segment she lists questions to help you remember what might have been going on in your life. She has more than 400 questions throughout the book.

Start with these prompts

Prepare nine pieces of paper or computer files, each with one of Spence's major life segments at the top, or whatever segments fit your memoir's purpose. In each segment write a brief line or two about activities you were involved in during that time. Your list could include a handful of activities or dozens. Don't write complete sentences or paragraphs and don't try to write a story; just bits of information you will refer to later when writing your stories.

Here are a few prompts to get your juices flowing:

- Old family photographs
- School yearbooks
- Travel photos

- What you were doing when big news events occurred
- Your first car wreck
- When you learned to ride a bicycle
- Letters from family and friends
- Family Bible
- Newspaper on the day you were born or other dates you select; search your browser for newspaper sites
- Family heirlooms: jewelry, books, furniture, clothing, dishes, and so forth
- Names of family members and friends
- Persons who most influenced you, for better or worse
- Those who guided your faith journey
- Firsts: first date, first learned to drive, first job, first child, and so forth
- Accomplishments and failures with lessons learned
- Saddest and happiest events
- Serious illness
- Death of a loved one
- Treasured friendships
- Friendships gone bad

Expand your opportunities to remember by exploring memory joggers with your senses: hearing, sight, touch, smell, and taste. Revisit places of your childhood, adolescence, or young adulthood. Spend time in a familiar place every day discovering your memory joggers—could be ten minutes, twenty minutes, forty-five minutes, or whatever works for you.

See **Memory Joggers** in **Resources** near the end of this book.

5. **Write in your natural voice, as though you were telling a story to a friend.**
Students in my life story writing classes frequently say, "I'm not a writer."

Stay with me, I'm going to get negative before I get positive.

I remember a scene in a movie from many years ago–can't remember the name of the movie–in which an Army drill instructor faced a group of new recruits for the first time. "I tell you now, you will never make it," the instructor barked.

Some established writers, agents, editors, and publishers tell aspiring writers the same thing, that writing what people want to read is hard, scary, and painful, and therefore newbies won't make it.

Consider these
Harper Lee, Pulitzer Prize winner for *To Kill a Mockingbird* published in 1960: "I wouldn't go through the pressure and publicity I went through with *To Kill a Mockingbird* for any amount of money." It was her only published book until *Go Set a Watchman* in 2015. *Watchman*, on which *Mockingbird* was based, was completed in the 1950s and never published until after the draft manuscript was discovered in 2014.

Michael Perry, author of three bestselling memoirs: "I just wrote and wrote and wrote for years, and then one day (after nearly a decade of writing every day and submitting work every month) the marbles aligned, not that the metaphor is perfect. I'm still trying to keep those marbles in line, and the table is forever tipping."

Paul Gallico (1897-1976), novelist and sportswriter: "It is only when you open your veins and bleed onto the page a little that you establish contact with your reader."

Susannah Breslin, short-story writer: "This is your roulette wheel, and when it lands on every number but the one you picked, and you realize that after years of work, you haven't made more than a pittance at what you thought would be your new career, you will call it a day."

How do you counter such negativity? Your image of what a writer should be may be skewed to unreal expectations. In the end, you need to be you. You need to write your life story the way you remember events and how they influenced you, without being restrained by arbitrary standards of so-called experts.

Don't try to be a writer

This doesn't mean you abandon effective storytelling techniques, good grammar, and proper punctuation. Learn your craft, and then you can break the rules. Your finished product should be you, not Harper Lee, Michael Perry, Paul Gallico, or Susannah Breslin. On the other hand, it soothes me to know Paul Gallico told *New York Times Magazine*, "I'm a rotten novelist. I'm not even literary. I just like to tell stories."

Jeff Collins, columnist and storytelling coach for *Springfield News-Leader* in Missouri, wrote, "Even the best storytellers can't agree on basic rules of storytelling."

How do you be you? Rather than staring at a blank page or empty computer screen, struggling to write like a writer, try telling your story to a digital voice recorder. You can buy them for thirty dollars to more than $300. My thirty-dollar recorder does everything I need, and I've used it more than five years. I bought it with a cable to transfer recordings to my computer for easy access.

Tell your story into the recorder just as you would tell it to a friend. For my book with Dorsey Levell, *Dumb Luck or Divine Guidance: My 31 Years with the Council of Churches of the Ozarks*, we did a series of audio-recorded interviews which I then transcribed and edited. Dorsey is a great storyteller; he readily admits he is a much better storyteller than writer. Some who know him told us that reading our book was like having a cup of coffee with him and listening to his stories, exactly the result we wanted.

6. Freewrite without editing or censoring.

It's easy to be bogged down in too many details when writing the first draft of your life story.

"Wait a minute," you say. "My life is about the details."

Yes, but . . . (There is always a *but*, right? Some purists declare everything before *but* is erased in the mind of the reader or hearer. But, that's not today's topic.)

Yes, but notice these words in the opening statement: *bogged down, too many details, first draft*.

Writing and editing are different processes. I'll have more on editing in a later tip. When writing, you should have a first draft you clean up by adding, deleting, rearranging, clarifying, and re-purposing days or weeks after you wrote it. If you stop to do all those things while writing, you may never have a draft to finish.

Author Stephen Guise says, "*Vomit* out the words first, and *clean it up later.*"

Bozo and Cheerio Syndrome

Suppose you are writing about your twelfth birthday party at your grandparents' house. Your grandparents hired Bozo the clown and his dog Cheerio. You strike through *twelfth*; it was your eleventh birthday. You strike through *grandparents*; it was your uncle and aunt. Oh, and the clown's name was Cheerio and his dog was Bozo. You trash the whole thing until you can get it exactly right. You could go on like that and never write the story.

It's okay to make your first draft ugly. This is the hardest part of writing for me. I always want to do the Bozo/Cheerio routine, even though I know I shouldn't. Many writing gurus say write it and worry about fixing it later.

Also in your freewriting, don't try to censor yourself. Eliminate from your thoughts ideas such as this is not an interesting story, I don't want to hurt anyone's feelings, my family remembers it differently, this is too personal, I'm not a writer. Go ahead and write what you are feeling and decide later whether to include it or modify it. Open your thoughts to all possibilities.

William Zinsser Model

Now in his nineties, William Zinsser has had a distinguished career as columnist, university professor, freelance writer, and author of eighteen books including two on memoirs. In *On Writing Well*, he suggests this model for writing your memoir:

1. Write about one event today. You may write in longhand, on the computer, one page, or several pages, but write only one event. "Don't be impatient to write your 'mem-

oir'—the one you had in mind before you began," he says.

2. Tomorrow, write about another event. And the next day and the next until you have written thirty or sixty or ninety stories or whatever fits your purpose. Do not edit or arrange the stories as you write.

3. When you have written all you want, place all of the stories onto the floor or large table and arrange them in the order you prefer. Rewrite to your satisfaction.

Voilà, you wrote your memoir.

7. Open with action or something interesting.

When I was a boy in the 1940s, I enjoyed going to the ten-cent movie theater just off the public square in my hometown and watching black-and-white cowboy movies. My heroes included Johnny Mack Brown, Whip Wilson, Hopalong Cassidy, The Durango Kid, Red Ryder, and Lash LaRue. Sorry ladies, no female Western movie heroes back then. There was Judy Canova, but she was not in the same league as the men.

The Western movies of my youth often began with a stagecoach roaring down a dusty road, the bad guys chasing and shooting, the stagecoach guard lying on top and shooting back. Soon, the stagecoach was surrounded by the bandits. The guard would jump onto the horse of a bandit and they went tumbling down a hillside.

Flash forward to today's action-adventure movies—they usually begin with action, or a mystery that quickly leads to action.

How experts do it

Novelist James Patterson begins *I, Alex Cross* with a young woman wearing only underwear, running through woods, bullets whizzing past and being slapped and scratched by tree branches. She stumbles onto a rural road, flags down a man driving a pickup truck, and climbs into the cab.

"Don't let them get me," she says to the driver.

"Who?"

"The men."

"What men?"

"The men from the White House."

You *have* to turn the page.

Cultural historian Teva Scheer is author of *Governor Lady: The Life and Times of Nellie Taylor Ross*, the biography of America's first female governor (Wyoming). Scheer begins with seven-year-old Nellie and her family standing on the banks of the Missouri River near St. Joseph, watching their bluff-top house burn to the ground. Then she fills in the backstory.

How I do it

My brother and I are writing our family history. Suppose we began like this: "I was born July 29, 1939, in a house in Marshall, Missouri, the second of three boys." Duuull! And a sure-fire way to stop readers from turning the page, or even finishing the paragraph.

Instead, we start like this: "Dad never liked his given name, Aloysius Elias. 'What kind of parents give a name like that?' he said on several occasions. Parents of strong German heritage, we learned."

When I speak to groups, I start my talks with something that grabs attention, such as:

"I used to be a pretty nice guy until I started using computers."

"I don't like it. It's hard work, time consuming, boring, I would rather be doing something else, and there is nothing in the Bible about it."

Quotes from famous people can immediately establish rapport with your audience and set the tone for your stories. Here are several I've used:

"Don't be a 'writer.' Be writing." William Faulkner (1897-1962)

"To *get* what *you want, you* must first *help others get* what *they want*." Dale Carnegie (1888-1955)

"I retired 17 years ago and have been behind in my work ever since." Shirley Povich (1905-1998), sportswriter for the *Washington Post*

Whether it is the first chapter in your book or the eighth, begin with the action or something interesting. Your readers will love it.

8. Think of your memoir or life story as scenes in a movie.

I dislike movies with narrators. Yadda, yadda, yadda. Get on with the story fer cryin' out loud. Narration at the beginning signals I'm not going to like the movie, while narration later in the movie bogs down my interest. Narration instead of action is a roadblock to my enjoyment, whether it's words on the screen or voice over.

Synonyms for telling are narration and exposition. A certain amount of exposition is necessary to move your story along, but only the more important parts deserve longer expositions. The lifeblood of your story is interaction of characters. What did you do when they came into and went out of your life, and how did you feel about what occurred?

Only four scenes

Think of your life story as a series of scenes in a movie. In the movie business, big screen or television, writers put together stories using only four scenes. Wait a minute. How is that possible? Simple: The scenes are indoors night or day and outdoors night or day. That's it. Nothing else. Everything happens within the framework of those scenes.

In your life story, you may be an observer of a scene or you may be in the scene. Close your eyes and visually walk through the scene. Who are your characters? What are they feeling, doing, and saying? Where have they been? Where are they going? Why are they doing things? What results from their actions? When will they reveal their secrets? How are they going to get out of this mess?

Creative writing instructor Robert McKee, in *Story: Substance, Structure, Style and the Principles of Screenwriting*, his handbook on the craft: "Never force words into a character's mouth to tell the audience about world, history, or person. Rather show us honest, natural scenes in which human beings talk and behave in honest, natural ways . . . In other words, dramatize exposition."

Action scenes don't need words. In the movie *Jurassic Park*, characters seek safety inside a laboratory. The camera shows a bowl of motionless water on a lab table. Small ripples appear in the water and become increasingly stronger, low thumping noises get louder, then a dinosaur crashes into the lab. Jumped outta my seat!

Words on paper
Freelance editor and mentor Bobbie Christmas says this is telling: "Harry was nervous. He wondered if the police sketch looked so much like

him that he could be recognized." She says this is showing: "Harry raked his clammy hands against his jeans. He gawked at the bulletin board. The police sketch gazed back at him, his image exactly. He tugged at his collar, gulped, and glanced around to see if anybody recognized him."

Daniel Woodrell begins nearly every chapter of *Winter's Bone* describing a harsh Ozarks winter. His characters rely on winter settings:

"Weather burst on the woman's hat and shoulders, wet spray jumping. She touched Ree's hood, rapped knuckles against the ice to break it fine, and swiped the pieces away."

"Ree stomped the ice and it creaked but did not crack wide. She took another step, and another, then came back for the ax. She stood on the ice near the willow, raised the ax and put all her feelings into the whacks she delivered unto that pond."

"Black ice lay slick where the road bottomed, and the truck slid a surprise twist sideways and completed most of a circle before rubber found dry asphalt again and Gail yanked the squealing tires straight. She yelped and slowed fearfully to a shambling pace, then suddenly stopped altogether and sat trembling, overlooking a steep bank of scrub and a frozen cow pond."

Sorry to say, the movie version didn't do justice to Woodrell's winter scenes. Alas, the director didn't ask my advice.

9. Use dialogue to break up narrative and give authenticity to your stories.

Actress, author, health and beauty adviser Marilu Henner is among a handful of people in the world known to have superior autobiographical memory. She can recall the correct days of the week for holidays in just about any year of her life, what she had for dinner ten years ago, and the date and circumstances of each time she met someone.

Russian journalist Solomon Veniaminovich Shereshevsky (1886–1958) could hear a speech once and recite it word for word.

Memory expert Hideaki Tomoyori holds the world record for memorizing 40,000 digits of *pi*.

Stage actors memorize long lines of dialogue by associating key words, sentences, sounds, and images.

But how do life story writers remember exact words of conversations years after events? Some reviewers criticized Mary Karr for pages of dialogue in her memoir, *The Liars' Club*, saying they could not tell whether she was remembering or lying.

The whole truth (See chapter To Tell the Truth)

Truth is, life story writers don't remember exactly. They write the flavor or tenor of conversations that give the results they remember. More important than remembering exactly is remembering the truths and meanings of events.

Consider the Bible, which is top-of-the-food-chain for life story writing. Just about everything in the Bible is stories told from generation to generation before it was written. No video cameras, digital voice recorders, or journalists were on hand when events occurred. After the stories were first written they were copied and recopied many times in different languages before a committee assembled them into what we know as the Bible. Influence of the Holy Spirit *to the contrary notwithstanding* (politicians say that a lot), a friend of mine looks at that scenario this way, "I don't know whether everything in the Bible happened the way it was written, but I believe it's true."

When writing your life story, get as close as you can to the actual dialogue, but don't be concerned if you can't remember exactly. The results of your conversations, your feelings, what you did and learned are much more valuable than *exactly*.

Simple exercises

Kendra Bonnett and Matilda Butler, authors of *Rosie's Daughters*, suggest practicing your listening skills as a technique for improving your written dialogue: Go to a public place, listen to people talk, and make notes. Think about the meaning of the conversation, not the words, and write a commentary about the conversation.

Creative writing consultant Nancy Strauss: "Writing effective dialogue is a delicate art. You need to sound authentic, capture each character's voice. And you need to cut it at the right moments." Although you and I often may say *please, thank you, uh, I know, yeah, appreciate it,* and other trite words and phrases, when written they make dialogue cluttered and contrived. Strauss suggests eight exercises to practice writing dialogue. Find them at http://tinyurl .com/pfxuvyo.

Most real-life conversations are boring (think telephone calls). Your objective with dialogue in your life story is more than accurate quotes. It is relevant dialogue that tells readers important things about persons and story and keeps readers engaged. If it doesn't do that, then rewrite until it does. The next time you watch a television drama, pay attention to how the dialogue moves the story and tells you about characters.

10. **Give yourself permission to write about painful memories.**
I have no nasty secrets that, if revealed on the front page of a newspaper, would bring great pain to my wife, my children, my friends, or me. Embarrassment perhaps, but not pain.

I'm not a therapist, licensed or self-proclaimed. Therefore, I can't speak from personal experience. But I have learned from students, clients, friends, and professionals that writing a life story can be healing. If you are haunted by memories and secrets which have become burdens to your happiness, then writing your stories can bring release from your haunts.

Claim your experiences

"Secrets maintain a great power over us, and we are diminished by them," says Linda Joy Myers, therapist and author who founded the National Association of Memoir Writers. She says to release yourself from the past you must claim your own truths. "Your story is about you–told from your point of view. Your experiences belong to you, are unique to you, and you have a right to claim them, even if others disagree."

Author Jeff Goins says when we write about the painful parts it helps heal us, helps heal others, and helps heal the world. "Don't avoid painful writing," he says. "Don't procrastinate sharing your scars. Take an honest look inward and begin today. It may be the most courageous thing you've ever done."

In her memoir *Nowhere but Up*, Pattie Mallette tells of her alcoholic and abusive father, her drinking and drugs starting at age fourteen, her attempted suicide, being sexually molested so many times she thought it was normal to feel dirty and unloved, giving birth to an out-ofwedlock son and raising him in low-income housing. A neighbor helped with babysitting so she could get her high school diploma. And she found hope in Christianity, even though her faith is a bit shaky at times. Not familiar with the name Pattie Mallette? This should help: The full title of her memoir is *Nowhere but Up: The Story of Justin Bieber's Mom*. She was eighteen when she gave birth to him.

"Writing the book was part of my healing process," she told an interviewer. "There are parts that are still painful to go over."

Don't censor yourself

Write the painful parts of your life. Don't try to get it right the first time, just write. Don't censor yourself as you go along or you will end up talking yourself out of writing about the hurts. You can decide later whether to edit or include them.

Caution: Writing about your pain in itself is not a substitute for the guidance of a therapist or other professional, including a support group. Memoirist Sue William Silverman was in therapy much of her adult life, the result of sexual abuse by her father when she was a child. Her therapist repeatedly advised her to write about her experiences, but she could not until her parents died.

You have options. One, keep the painful memories locked inside so as not to hurt others and keep hurting yourself. Two, reveal and risk further pain to those you love who might think less of you or take their love from you. Three, write from the perspective of love and forgiveness rather than a victim; you will get through it, you will better understand who you are, and you will have greater respect for yourself.

11. **Ask a trusted friend to read your work and make suggestions.**
Let's say you finished writing your life story, or even several chapters, and you're feeling pretty good about it. Your stories are interesting, with lead sentences that grab a reader's attention. You ran the spelling and grammar check on your computer and all looks well. While you may not be ready to publish with a traditional big-name company, you are ready for the next step. What is the next step?

Defining the term

You likely wrote your life story for family and friends and not to become a best-selling author. You may be planning to take your manuscript to a local quick-print store, have it bound in spiral-notebook form on eight-and-a-half-by-eleven sheets, add a clear plastic cover for protection, and buy a dozen printed copies. Fine to do, but you also should do the best you can so your family and friends will not label you a careless, know-nothing amateur (in their minds, though they might not say that to your face).

The key is *trusted friend*—not your spouse, your children, your grandmother, or your best buddy from high school, college, work, or church, because they won't tell you the truth. They will pat you on the back and say how impressed they are you wrote a great book.

The trusted friend I recommend is someone with knowledge of writing. This could be an English or writing teacher, a published author, a person who makes a living editing a magazine or newspaper, or a member of a local writing group who is experienced at giving feedback; someone who will do the job as a special favor at no charge. At this point you are not seeking perfection; you are looking for impressions. Ask your friend how he/she feels about your stories. Do the stories make sense? Does the narrative flow evenly? Are the events in chronological order (unless you planned them to be out of order). Do not ask your friend to proofread or edit your manuscript; those are steps that will come later. You are looking only for friendly feedback, simple suggestions on how your manuscript could be improved.

Encourage your friend to comment along these lines:

"Seems to me this chapter would fit better earlier in the book."

"I think some dialogue would add interest to this section."

"You've told this story three times. How about thinking of other ways to include the same information?"

"Are you comfortable revealing details of this relationship?"

After Dorsey Levell and I reviewed our manuscript for *Dumb Luck or Divine Guidance,* we asked four people to look it over, none of whom was a professional proofreader or editor. Then we hired a professional to proofread and edit.

While you should review your own work, the challenge is you are so close to the writing and to the value of stories that influenced you that you are likely to miss the obvious and nuanced of form and clarity.

Check with your librarian for the name and contact of a writers' group near you. You usually can attend several times without joining, and I encourage you to join. Like-spirits can be a big help. Many writers' groups have critique sessions and some have mentoring programs, both free. Freelance writer Jan Fields has tips in "Starting a Critique Group" at http://tinyurl.com/ot42u7u. Search your browser using that name for similar resources.

12. Edit, edit, edit

I picked up a paperback in a friend's office. The 300-page book had dimensions of a sheet of copy paper. The author, a man in his eighties, spent a lifetime developing and promoting tourism in a popular area and wanted to share his experiences in book form as a lasting legacy. In the introduction, he noted that family members, friends, and a professional writer read his manuscript and suggested changes. However, he thought his book was just fine with colloquialisms and homespun humor and decided against making changes.

His introduction and the rest of the book were riddled with misspelled words, grammatical errors, and imprecise sentence structures. What he took for local flavor came across as his lack of education and little consideration of readers. His motivation seemed on target, but his writing lacked quality. He probably thought readers would see his accomplishments as wonderful–they were wonderful and numerous–and overlook his technical mistakes. However, by writing poorly, he drew my attention from his achievements.

You may be motivated to write your memoir or life story by several strong desires: leave a legacy, tell of exciting travels, heal wounds, share your spiritual testimony, pass along your business wisdom, or dozens of other reasons. Regardless of motivation, you should strive for two outcomes: readers view you as credible and readers enjoy your story. Note the focus on readers. You achieve those outcomes by the quality of your writing. You achieve quality by proofreading, editing, and formatting your manuscript. Too many beginning authors think finishing their manuscripts renders them done and they go directly to publishing. Not a good idea.

How-to author and memoir-writing coach Sharon Lippincott: "Write like nobody will ever read it. Edit like the whole world will."

Blogger Derbhile Dromey: "Good editing is a bit like gardening. You cut back the dead wood to allow the flowers to bloom."

Author Jeff Goins: "It's never beautiful at the outset. Before your work can reach its potential, it will first have to be bad."

Ernest Hemingway (1899-1961) said he rewrote the ending of *Farewell to Arms* thirty-nine times, "To get the words right."

These experts are saying simple proofreading is not enough. Your computer's spellchecker will find some spelling and grammar errors, not all of which you will agree are errors, but it will not help find your emotional story nor similar-sounding words spelled differently. You will have to reread your manuscript several times and rewrite sections several times in order to get satisfying results your audience will want to read.

Profile of a book editor
Long ago, in a galaxy far away, staff book editors were an essential part of traditional publishing at the big publishing houses. Their job was to take a manuscript with potential and polish it

into a sales-ready product. Not anymore. With the explosion of self-publishing and print-on-demand vendors, publishers are more discriminating in what they will consider. Authors no longer can expect publishers to clean up their manuscripts. In order to get past the gatekeepers of traditional publishers, authors have to have more than a great story. They must submit manuscripts that need few or no corrections.

A professional book editor will:
1. Check for spelling, grammar, and punctuation errors.
2. Spot conflicting sections.
3. Identify sections needing improved flow and feel of the story.
4. Flag facts that need checking.
5. Prepare an index.
6. Design the interior, including layout, font, and text size.
7. Select illustrations.
8. Secure permissions for using material from other sources.

Some of these require individual expertise, and teams of editors may work on the process. With few exceptions, you are expected to do these tasks, or see they get done, before you submit your manuscript.

How to find an independent professional editor

Ask your librarian for the name and contact person of a writers' group near you. One or more professional editors may be members of the group. Ask for credentials and references.

Talk with the head of the English Department at a college or university in your area. Some institutions have literary publishing divisions whose staff may be available for outside editing work, or they could recommend a contractor with whom they have had success. If a student or college employee is suggested, be sure their skills and results can be proven.

Search the web for freelance editors. Talk with them and get references of satisfied and unsatisfied customers. Search for self-editing methods to give yourself a head start on the process. For fee purposes, editors often divide their work into two parts: proofreading and editing. Proofreading–sometimes called light editing–involves spelling, grammar, and punctuation. Editing and heavy editing involve story structure, rewriting, rearranging, and deleting portions of the manuscript. Steve Wiegenstein, author of *Slant of Light,* says he removed the first five chapters to shorten the length at the request of his publisher. He didn't delete the chapters; he saved them and inserted portions elsewhere.

See **Book Editors** under **Resources** in the following section.

NOTES

RESOURCES

Suggested Reading

Visit your library, bookstore, or online retailer for books on how to write memoirs or life stories, life story accounts, and reference books on writing. Before tackling the how-to books, find a few life stories you think you might enjoy and read them for ideas. This will help you get a handle on the techniques and emotions of the authors. The ones you like best are the ones that draw you into the stories.

How-to Books
I reviewed these books on my blog, www.wayne groner.com.

101 Best Beginnings Ever Written, Barnaby Conrad (Quill Driver Books, 2009)

Breathe Life into Your Life Story, Dawn Thurston and Morris Thurston (Signature Books, 2007)

The Complete Idiot's Guide to Writing a Memoir, Victoria Costello (Alpha/Penguin, 2011)

Fearless Confessions: A Writer's Guide to Memoir, Sue William Silverman (University of Georgia Press, 2009)

Heart and Craft of Lifestory Writing: How to Transform Memories Into Meaningful Stories, Sharon M. Lippincott (Lighthouse Point Press, 2007)

Legacy: A Step-by-step Guide to Writing Personal History, Linda Spence (Swallow Press/Ohio University Press, 1997)

On Writing Well, 30th Anniversary Edition: The Classic Guide to Writing Nonfiction, William Zinsser (Harper Paperbacks, 2006)

You Can Write Your Family History, Sharon Debartolo Carmack (Genealogical Publishing Company, 2009)

Reference Books

The Blue Book of Grammar and Punctuation, Jane Straus, Lester Kaufman, Tom Stern (Jossey-Bass, 2014)

The Chicago Manual of Style, 16th Edition, University of Chicago Press Staff (University of Chicago Press, 2010)

The Emotion Thesaurus: A Writer's Guide to Character Expression, Angela Ackerman and Becca Puglisi

(CreateSpace Independent Publishing Platform, 2012)

Oxford American Writer's Thesaurus, Third Edition, compiled by Christine L. Lindberg (Oxford University Press, 2012)

Why You Should Write Your Life Story Now

"Refute These 14 Reasons Not to Write Your Memoirs," http://tinyurl.com/nesus7s. I can't remember, I'm too old, I'm too young, nothing interesting has happened to me, and ten more excuses Jerry Waxler shoots holes through. Waxler is founder of *Memory Writers Network* and co-founder of *Lifewriters Forum*.

Write Your Life Stories.com. First seven lessons of an online course free by Sheila Ellison, teacher, editor, coach, and bestselling author of ten books.

Telling Your Story, http://tinyurl.com/qay8whx. Do it now before memories fade and while people are still alive. Tips and resources by personal historian Pat McNeese.

"Writers Workshop Series: Writing Your Memoir," http://tinyurl.com/nvdm5lb. Seven tips by Carolyn Oravitz, teacher and freelance writer.

"So, You Want to Publish Your Memoir," http://tinyurl.com/qetdt3c. Fern Reiss on writing about a high-conflict family member.

"How to Write an Autobiography,"
http://tinyurl.com/3qepoof. Four major steps by the
writers at wikiHow.

"How to Write a Memoir,"
http://tinyurl.com/qampche. Be yourself, speak
freely, and think small, by William Zinsser, author
and teacher. How do you remember everything that
happened? You don't have to says Zinsser. Just focus
on key events you feel were important to you.

Membership Organizations

A great way to keep up with the trends in life writing
and stay current with new and established methods
is to join an organization. Much of the information
is free, and you can interact with writers who have
done what you've done or who are moving along at
your pace. Member benefits include support, networking, conferences, critiquing, and workshops.
Check with your librarian for a local group near you.
Membership fees vary.

Online forums for life story writers can help get your
writing juices going. You may participate in the discussions or choose to lurk. Problem solving is a major focus of these forums. Enter into your browser's
search field the words *writers forum, nonfiction writers forum, memoir writers forum, or life story writers
forum*. Lots of choices will come up. Test drive several to find one or more that work best for you. Forums are free.

The following organizations have members throughout the world. Membership fees are annual in U.S. dollars and subject to change.

Association of Personal Historians

http://www.personalhistorians.org/

Purpose - Advance the profession of helping individuals, organizations, and communities preserve their life stories.

Services - Educational, training, and networking opportunities to help professional personal historians, from beginners to advanced, build their personal history businesses, member web directory, regional events, annual conference, APH store.

Membership - $200. Open to any interested in per

Biographers International Organization

http://biographersinternational.org/

Purpose - Represent the everyday interests of practicing biographers: those who have published the stories of real lives, and those working on biographies in every medium from print to film.

Services - Member web directory, annual BIO Award for lifetime contribution to biography, annual conference, and monthly newsletter.

Membership Levels:

Active - $45 to $150 based on annual writing income from biography. For those who are writing, filming, recording, or otherwise producing a biography.

Associate - $30. For anyone interested in the craft and art of biography.

Affiliate - $250. For corporations, companies, and firms wishing to provide financial support to BIO.

International Auto/Biography Association

http://iaba-americas.org/

Purpose - Broaden the world vision of auto/biographers, scholars, and readers; deepen the cross-cultural understanding of self, identity and experience; and carry on global dialogues on life writing.

Services - Biennial conference in exotic world locations, periodic newsletter.

Membership - Membership fee not required.

International Society of Family History Writers and Editors

http://www.isfhwe.org/

Purpose - Encourage excellence in writing and editorial standards in genealogical publishing. This embraces all media, including newspapers, magazines, newsletters, professional journals, books (including compiled family histories), online columns, society and personal websites, web logs (blogs), and broadcast journalism of all kinds.

Services - Quarterly newsletter, annual writing competition, annual conference, links to members' publications and websites.

Membership - $15. Open to anyone involved in genealogy columns and articles or writing about family history. This includes present and potential columnists, writers, and editors, as well as publishers, broadcasters, and webmasters for genealogical and historical societies.

National Association of Memoir Writers
http://namw.org/
Purpose - Help memoir writers feel empowered with purpose and energy to begin and develop their life stories into a publishable memoir, whether in essay form, a book, a family legacy, or to create a blog.
Services - Workshops; tele-seminars; interviews with writers and experts in the area of memoir, writing skills, therapeutic writing, spiritual autobiography, and healing through writing personal, authentic stories. Free subscription to monthly email newsletter, no membership required.
Membership - $149. Open to anyone interested in memoir writing.

Memory Joggers

"Oral History Interviews, Questions and Topics," http://www.jewishgen.org/infofiles/Quest.html

Kindred Keepsakes, http://tinyurl.com/ndvc564

"The Life Story Interview," http://tinyurl.com/oox8fsr

Memory List Question Book, http://tinyurl.com/qgz4vs3

"Make a Memory Book Scrapbook," http://tinyurl.com/cenznyr

A History of Me, http://tinyurl.com/nlsuey9
Writing Your Life: An Easy-to-Follow Guide to Writing an Autobiography, http://tinyurl.com/plsm8ou

Find dozens more resources by searching your browser for *memoir writing prompts, memoir writing questions,* or *memoir memory joggers.*

Free Newsletters

Newsletters by email are among the quickest and easiest ways to get free help. Written by professionals who have done just what you are doing, the newsletters provide tips for writing, organizing, editing, and publishing, as well as encouragement and support. Online newsletters may include:

- Tips to get you started and keep you moving.
- Motivating articles.
- Links to other resources.
- Information on classes and workshops.
- Methods to make the best use of your time.
- Tools for better storytelling.
- Connections with other life story writers.
- Techniques that work to unblock stalled thinking.
- Assistance growing your life story writing business.
- Special offers at reduced prices.

Newsletters from the following include information on life story writing or on general writing. Some are weekly and some monthly; some may offer to sell you services or products.

Explore Writing, http://tinyurl.com/ogxr6to
Extraordinary Lives, http://tinyurl.com/ohscu5a

Footprints Writing Clubs,
http://tinyurl.com/ptwems8

Grammar and Composition Guide,
http://grammar.about.com/

Summertime Publishing,
http://tinyurl.com/olvw6ok. Free report, "How to Write Your Life Story, The Inside Secrets," when you subscribe to the newsletter.

Kimberly Powell's Genealogy Guide,
http://genealogy.about.com/

Laura Davis, Healing Words That Change Lives,
http://lauradavis.net/

National Association of Memoir Writers,
http://namw.org/. Free report, "Begin Your Memoir Today!" when you subscribe to the newsletter.

White Smoke, http://tinyurl.com/yb32zcz

The Muffin–Fresh News Daily,
http://tinyurl.com/2e7lr4r
Writer's Digest, http://www.writersdigest.com/

Writing-World, http://tinyurl.com/pehllhb

Book Editors

Galleycat, http://tinyurl.com/og6l4rs, "Best Book Editors on Twitter," with links to and comments from the editors.

Editors Only, http://tinyurl.com/ng8hj83, a directory of professional associations for editors.
Editing fees vary with skills and experiences of editors and the amount of work they do. Some charge by the project, page, or hour. The Editorial Freelancers Association lists common editorial rates, http://www.the-efa.org/res/rates.php.

Search your browser for *freelance editors* or *proofreaders*.

You can and should do a lot of the editing and proofing before you hire a professional. "What! I have to do it myself *and* hire someone?" Yup, if you want to do it right. A few tips:

"Self-Editing Basics: 10 Simple Ways to Edit Your Own Book," http://tinyurl.com/q99utov.

"How I Self-Edit My Novels: 15 Steps From First Draft to Publication," http://tinyurl.com/oe2xhra.
This one will wear you out, but it gets the job done. Applies to life story as well as novels.
"What to Look for When Editing Your Manuscript," http://tinyurl.com/oq6wrpz

Although the World Wide Web has thousands of articles on self-editing and professional editing, if you master the processes in the three articles above, you'll be okay.

FINALLY

I started this book with a quote from Mark Twain and will end with another: "I like a good story well told. That is the reason I am sometimes forced to tell them myself."

You know your story better than anyone. Now is the time to tell it.

NOTES

BOOKS BY THE AUTHOR

Wayne E. Groner

Witnesses of Hope, Faith, Love and Healing, compiler and editor (Community of Christ Chapel for Peace, 2012)

A Guide to Writing Your Memoir or Life Story: Tools, Tips, Methods, and Examples (Paperback-Press Publishing, 2015)

Wayne E. Groner and Dorsey E. Levell

The Pastor's Guide to Fund-Raising Success (Bonus Books, 1999. Republished by Taylor Trade Publishing, 2003)

Dumb Luck or Divine Guidance: My 31 Years with the Council of Churches of the Ozarks, Dorsey E. Levell as told to Wayne E. Groner (Council of Churches of the Ozarks, 2009)

NOTES

NOTES

NOTES

NOTES

NOTES